Lord, I Need Help!
Walking with the Holy Spirit

Book Two

Walking with Jesus

Becoming the Best Me I Can Be

Pamela D White

All scripture quotations, unless otherwise indicated, are taken from the Holy Bible, **New King James Version©**. Copyright © 1982 by Thomas Nelson, Inc. Used by permission. All rights reserved.

Scripture quotations marked NIV are taken from the Holy Bible, **New International Version** ®, NIV ®. Copyright © 1973, 1978, 1984 by **Biblica, Inc.® Used by permission. All rights reserved worldwide.**

Scripture quotations marked NASB are taken from the Holy Bible, **New American Standard Bible®**, Copyright © 1960, 1971, 1977, 1995, 2020 by The Lockman Foundation. All rights reserved.

Scripture quotations marked AMP are taken from the Holy Bible, **Amplified**, copyright © 2015 by The Lockman Foundation, La Habra, CA 90631. All rights reserved. For Permission To Quote information visit http://www.lockman.org/

Scripture quotations marked ESV are taken from the ESV® Bible (The Holy Bible, **English Standard Version®**). ESV® Text Edition: 2016. Copyright © 2001 by Crossway, a publishing ministry of Good News Publishers. The ESV® text has been reproduced in cooperation with and by permission of Good News Publishers. Unauthorized reproduction of this publication is prohibited. All rights reserved.

Scripture quotations marked NLT are taken from the Holy Bible, **New Living Translation,** copyright © 1996, 2004, 2015 by Tyndale House Foundation. Used by permission of Tyndale House Publishers, Inc., Carol Stream, Illinois 60188. All rights reserved.

Scripture quotations marked MSG are taken from **THE MESSAGE**, copyright © 1993, 2002, 2018 by Eugene H. Peterson. Used by permission of NavPress. All rights reserved. Represented by Tyndale House Publishers, Inc.

Scripture quotations marked AKJV are taken from the Holy Bible, **Authorized King James Version**, The Authorized (King James) Version of the Bible ('the KJV'), the rights in which are vested in the Crown in the United Kingdom, is reproduced here by permission of the Crown's patentee, Cambridge University Press. The Cambridge KJV text, including paragraphing, is reproduced here by permission of Cambridge University Press.

Scripture quotations marked KJV are taken from the Holy Bible**, King James Version**.

A publication of Blooming Desert Ministries

ISBN 978-1-7370802-2-0 (sc print)
ISBN 978-1-7370802-3-7 (ebook)

Printed in the United States of America
Copyright © 2021 by Pamela D White
All Rights Reserved.

IngramSparks Publishing (Ingram: Lightning Source, LLC)

One Ingram Blvd., La Vergne, TN 37086

Publishing Note: Publishing style capitalizes certain pronouns in Scriptures that refer to the Father, Son, and Holy Spirit, and may differ from other publishing styles. **All emphasis in the Scriptures' quotations is the authors.** The name satan and related names are not capitalized as the author's preference not to acknowledge him, even though it violates grammatical rules.

No part of this book may be reproduced or transmitted in any form or by any means, electronic or mechanical – including photocopying, recording, or by any information storage and retrieval system – without permission in writing from the publisher. Please direct inquires to PDW Publications.

Dedication

This book series is dedicated to you.

Everyone has opportunities to become a better version of themselves. My prayer is that this book series helps you on that journey. The Lord loves you so much He desires an intimate relationship with you. You are special to Him and He loves spending time with you. Walking and talking with Jesus every day should be the norm, not the exception. Life can bring difficult circumstances and situations. When you walk with Jesus, life events, are not only manageable but can be turned for your good.

"And we know that all things work together for good to those who love God, to those who are the called according to His purpose," Romans 8:28.

Come with me into this exploration of how you can develop a relationship with Jesus and walk with Him every day. This is an opportunity to become a better you.

Acknowledgments

The Great Commission given by our Lord and Savior Jesus Christ noted in Matthew 28:16-20 is my inspiration for this publication. Verses 19-20 state, *"Go therefore and make disciples of all the nations, baptizing them in the name of the Father and of the Son and of the Holy Spirit, teaching them to observe all things that I have commanded you; and lo, I am with you always, even to the end of the age."* This verse is the very basis for missionary work all over the globe. I have been blessed to be able to serve in a few of those missions. Missions are an amazing experience. I came to realize though that everyone cannot always do all the parts commanded in these verses. I can't always go. I didn't often get to baptize. What I realized was that I can do my part in teaching to observes the truths of the Scriptures. My desire to fulfill the teaching part of the Great Commission was the inspiration for this work. My pastor, Bishop Larry Taylor, and First Lady Desetra Taylor allowed our church to use these Bible studies in our New Life Discipleship classes for nearly twenty years. The work has also been used in prison ministries in central Illinois for as many years. The teaching has proven effective in changing many lives and discipling the children of God. Thank you, Bishop and First Lady, for teaching a balanced spiritual and natural life so I could complete this project and see the impact of the work on people's lives.

Bishop positioned me to be the director of New Life Ministries Discipleship for several years. New Life classes were designed to teach those new to Christianity or new to the church the foundational truths needed to build a solid life in Christ. During that time, this work was fine-tuned with the help and input from the dedicated, gifted, and anointed New Life teachers Minister Retta Smith, Minister James Smith, Minister Debby Henkel, Dr. Terry Husband, Minister Char-Michelle McDowell, Minister Yvonne Smith, Minister Herbert Smyer, and Professor Susan Gibson along with the encouragement and guidance of Dr. Chequita Brown and community service advocate Minister Patricia Turner. I also want to give a shout-out to Dr. Wanda Turner, nationally acclaimed minister, teacher, prophet, life coach, mentor, and best-selling author, who continued to encourage me to just publish the thing! Thanks to all of you. Each of you has made a significant impact on my life.

My dear friend and mentor, First Lady Marshell Wickware, supported the project and pushed me to publish it for years. Thanks for not giving up on me!

My life-long friend, Robin McClallen, thank you for all your support, input, and encouraging me to publish something. You have been instrumental in making me an author.

A special thanks to my husband, Brian K. White, for his patience and prayers as I spent hours and hours researching, writing, and rewriting. Thanks, BW!

Most of all thank you to the Holy Spirit and my Lord and Savior Jesus Christ. I present this work in obedience and honor to You.

Contents

Introduction	11
Father, Son, and Holy Spirit—Divine Trinity	15
God the Father	15
God the Son	17
God the Holy Spirit	18
Baptism in the Holy Spirit	23
Getting to Know the Holy Spirit	29
Attributes of the Holy Spirit	29
Personality of the Holy Spirit	31
Nature of the Holy Spirit	32
Works of the Holy Spirit	35
Filled With the Holy Spirit	43
Tools to Live Holy Through the Holy Spirit	51
References	53
Stepping Stones	55
Lord, I Need Help!	57
Glossary	59
About the Author	65

Lord, I Need Help!
Walking with the Holy Spirit

OBJECTIVE

This lesson brings conscious awareness of the nature and works of the Holy Spirit by exploring His presence in both the Old and New Testaments. We will review biblical evidence of the Holy Spirit, gain an understanding of the Divine Trinity's existence, and receive tips on how to embrace the Holy Spirit in all aspects of everyday life.

MEMORY VERSES

"But the Comforter, which is the Holy Ghost, whom the Father will send in my name, he shall teach you all things, and bring all things to your remembrance, whatsoever I have said to you," John 14:26 KJV.

"This I say then, "Walk in the Spirit, and you shall not fulfill the lust of the flesh," Galatians 5:16 KJV.

Lord, I Need Help!

A. Father, Son, Holy Spirit - Divine Trinity

    a. God the Father

    b. God the Son

    c. God the Holy Spirit

B. Baptism in the Holy Spirit

    a. What is Baptism in the Holy Spirit and Why Do I Need it?

C. Getting to Know the Holy Spirit

    a. Attributes of the Holy Spirit

    b. Personality of the Holy Spirit

    c. Nature of the Holy Spirit

D. Works of the Holy Spirit

E. Filled with the Holy Spirit. What Does that Look Like for Me?

F. Tools to Live Holy through the Holy Spirit

    a. Read the Bible and meditate on Scriptures

    b. Prayer

    c. Fasting

    d. Fellowshipping with Believers

    e. Maintain Good Works

Book Two

Lord, I Need Help!

Walking with the Holy Spirit

Introduction

First, let me introduce you to the Holy Spirit. The Holy Spirit is one of the three entities in the Divine Trinity. The concept of the Trinity can be difficult to grasp. If there is one God, then who is Jesus and who is the Holy Spirit? So many questions arise regarding the Trinity. I'm will not dissect and get into a huge discussion of Trinity. Let's just say that it's hard to understand and as you grow in Christ, as your relationship with Christ develops and matures, three in One becomes more normal and more comfortable. As you meditate on the Word and enter into conversation with the Lord in your prayer time, you will begin to 'get it.' I'm pretty sure we won't fully grasp the full concept of Father, Son, and Holy Spirit until we get to heaven. In the meantime, I'll share what I know at this point in time.

The Holy Spirit is an intelligent personage who has self-consciousness and freedom. In the Old Testament, the Hebrew word for the Spirit is *ru-*

wach (roo'-akh), which means "wind". The Greek word used in the New Testament for Spirit is *pneuma* (pnyoo'-mah), which means "breath" or "breeze". The Holy Spirit is the Breath of God. We first meet the Holy Spirit in the first chapter of Genesis. *"In the beginning God created the heavens and the earth. The earth was without form, and void; and darkness was on the face of the deep. And the Spirit of God was hovering over the face of the waters,"* Genesis 1:1-2. If you notice in this very first verse of the Bible is the Father and the Spirit working together. God spoke creation while the Spirit hovered, working the creation. In verse 26, Father God speaks and says, *"Let us make man in Our image."* Who is us? 'Us' is the Father, the Son, and the Holy Spirit. Just a few verses later in Genesis 2:7, we see God breathing the breath of life into the man He had created out of the dust of the ground and that mass of mud lived. How amazing! That is the Holy Spirit—**The Breath of God**. Father, Son, and Holy Spirit are united in the oneness of the Godhead. Without the Holy Spirit, the Breath of God, you do not exist as a living, breathing being.

Here is a simplified example of the Trinity or the Godhead. Many times, God provides the simplest pieces of creation to better understand the deep truths of God. We often try to make God into some incomprehensible complicated being, but when we turn off the logic and analytics, we can better understand who He really is. We can see God's truths in the simplest things. Consider an egg. Just a simple egg. It has three parts: a shell, the white, and a yolk. All three parts are part of the egg. You ask for an egg white omelet and even though it's only one part of the egg it's still an egg. Separate the yolk from the rest of the egg to use in a recipe; it's still an egg. Blow the white and the yolk out of the egg to make super-special colored egg crafts; it's still an egg. Three parts and still one egg. Together it's an egg. Separate, still an egg. This is how the Godhead

Trinity works. Each person of the Godhead is equally important and equally God. They have different functions, but the same purpose. They hold the same characteristics and yet are unique in their relationship with humankind.

Another natural example to help explain Father, Son, and Holy Spirit is water. We can see water in three forms - liquid, solid, and vapor (or gas). Each form has a different function and appearance but does not cease to be H_2O. Whether it's steam from the kettle, ice cubes from the freezer, or liquid in the bathtub, it's still water. The Father, Son, and Holy Spirit are all God with different functions or roles. To better understand the Holy Spirit, let's look at each member of the Godhead, Father, Son, and Holy Spirit.

Father, Son, and Holy Spirit— Divine Trinity

The unity of three persons in One God defines the Holy Trinity. In order to comprehend the unity of three persons, you must understand who each of them is. Let's talk about the Father, Daddy, Abba, Jehovah Elohim, the Mighty God.

GOD THE FATHER

The Father is the one that first had you in mind. He created you and made a plan for your life. When sin tried to kill you and condemn you, He instituted a plan to redeem you from sin, pay your ransom, and declare your righteousness. Sin separates you from God, but Father God justified you by His grace through Jesus Christ, providing a bridge so you have free access to His throne and His ear. *"For all have sinned, and come short of the glory of God; Being justified freely by his grace through the redemption that is in Christ Jesus: Whom God has set forth to be a propitiation through faith in his blood, to declare his righteousness for the remission of sins that are past, through the forbearance of God,"* Romans 3:23-25 KJV.

The **FATHER ADOPTS YOU**. He wants you to be part of His family so much that He legally made you His own. This puts you in the position of a son or daughter and makes you a legal heir of everything that is the Father's. If He has it, then it's already yours because you are His child. *"Therefore, dear brothers and sisters, you have no obligation to do what your sinful nature urges you to do. For if you live by its dictates, you will die. But if through the power of the Spirit you put to death the deeds of your sinful nature, you will live. For all who are led by the Spirit of God are children of God. So you have not received a spirit that makes you fearful slaves. Instead, you received God's Spirit when he adopted you as his own children. Now we call him, "Abba, Father." For his Spirit joins with our spirit to affirm that we are God's children. And since we are his children, we are his heirs. In fact, together with Christ we are heirs of God's glory. But if we are to share his glory, we must also share his suffering,"* Romans 8:12-17.

Father gives forgiveness and delivers you from the guilt of sin. He didn't have to forgive you and certainly didn't have to deliver you. Father could have let you die in your sin and started over with a new creation. He even made this suggestion to Moses, so He thought about starting over with a new creation for a minute. It was His love for you that put aside that thought and offered you forgiveness instead of annihilation; Father God had every right to destroy man, including you and me. Instead, He let that go and loved instead. He offered forgiveness and a life with Him eternally. *"And be you kind one to another, tenderhearted, forgiving one another, even as God for Christ's sake has forgiven you,"* Ephesians 4:32 AKJV.

God the Son

Now let's talk about the Son, Jesus. He is the King of Kings, the Lord of Lords, and the Name above all names. Everything the Father has is His and everything the Father does He can do. Everything the Father thinks, He knows, and does. His purpose is 100% the same as the Father's. His role is just a little different.

Jesus redeems the sinner, you and me, from the bondage of sin by His sacrificial ransom. The payment was His own innocent, sinless blood, which He paid in full on the cross.

Remember, sin separates you from God. There is nothing you can do to bridge that gulf. Jesus reconciles you by restoring the relationship between man and God. Jesus and His work on the cross create the bridge to bring you back into a full relationship with Father God. *"For as much as you know that you were not redeemed with corruptible things, as silver and gold, from your vain conversation received by tradition from your fathers; but with the precious blood of Christ, as of a lamb without blemish and without spot,"* 1 Peter 1:18-19 AKJV.

As your propitiation, Jesus satisfies the anger of God toward practicing sin, which makes divine forgiveness possible. He appeased the anger of the Father. Father God doesn't want to be angry, but sin angers Him. However, **Father God loved you so much** that He sent Jesus to pay the price for your sin so the relationship between the Father and you experience restoration.

"Herein is love, not that we loved God, but that he loved us, and sent his Son to be the propitiation for our sins," 1 John 4:10 KJV.

GOD THE HOLY SPIRIT

Now, you know a little about the Father and Jesus the Son. It's time to talk about the Holy Spirit. The rest of this lesson talks about the Holy Spirit's attributes, characteristics, and position with the Father and the Son. (Just a brief note, we often refer to the Holy Spirit with the pronoun 'He' which I also use because Jesus refers to the Holy Spirit as 'he' such as in John 14 and 15. Some interpretations call the Holy Spirit the Holy Ghost. He is not a ghost in the Casper kind of way. The word interpreted ghost is the same word interpreted spirit—the Greek word 'pneuma') Before we get too deep into who the Holy Spirit is, let's take a brief look at His position in the Godhead trinity. An important thing to remember about the Holy Spirit is that His presence in your life is a gift. You should never take Him for granted.

"Then Peter said to them, "Repent, and let every one of you be baptized in the name of Jesus Christ for the remission of sins; and you shall receive the gift of the Holy Spirit," Acts 2:38.

The Father has a will that He expects you to seek after and follow. Sometimes it is difficult to know what that will is for your life. The Father sent the Holy Spirit to help you institute and follow the will of God. A Greek word for Holy Spirit found in the New Testament is the word Paraclete meaning "one called alongside of". The Holy Spirit comes alongside of you to be your partner through life. He is the Help you need to get through life's situations and circumstances. The Apostle John called the Holy Spirit the Comforter (parakletos), your help, your teacher, the link to the Father's will.

"But the Comforter, which is the Holy Ghost, whom the Father will send in my name, He shall teach you all things, and bring all things to your remembrance, whatever I have said to you," John 14:26 KJV.

As mentioned previously, the Holy Spirit appears in both the Old and New Testaments (*see Scriptures noted at the end of the paragraph*). He didn't suddenly appear in the book of Acts. He was present throughout the Bible. The Holy Spirit's name perfectly describes His character. He is holy, and He is spirit. The definition of **'Holy'** is to be pure, clean, separated, consecrated, sacred **(H6944 - qodesh - Strong's Hebrew Lexicon (KJV), 2020)**. The definition of **'Spirit'** is the manifestation of a presence, power, influence, or wisdom; no physical body, but can manifest itself with or without a physical or tangible being **(H7307 - ruwach - Strong's Hebrew Lexicon (KJV), 2020)**. As noted previously, we sometimes refer to the Spirit of God as the Holy Ghost. The Greek word 'pneuma' that was discussed at the beginning of this chapter is the word sometimes interpreted as ghost. Today's definition of a ghost is the apparition of a dead person. The Holy Spirit is not an apparition, and He was never a human, nor was He ever dead. He is very much alive. The term in New Testament times meant without bodily form as wind. Again, He is the Breath of God.

Scriptural examples of the Holy Spirit's presence in the Old Testament

Genesis 1:2, 6:3
Job 32:8, 33:4
Judges 6:34

Nehemiah 9:20, 30
Judges 3:10
Exodus 35:30-36:1

Exodus 31:3
1 Samuel 16:13
Judges 14:6
Psalm 143:10

Scriptural examples of the Holy Spirit's presence in the New Testament

Romans 15:13
John 3:6-8
Matthew 12:28
2 Corinthians 13:14
Romans 8:2-6
John 6:63
1 Corinthians 2:9-11
Matthew 10:20
Luke 24:45-4
1 Corinthians 12:11
Acts 2:1-5
2 Peter 1:21
1 John 2:19-27

He should be respected and honored. The Holy Spirit is the **MANIFEST PRESENCE AND POWER OF GOD** that comes pure, clean, and sacred. The Holy Spirit is God in you that enables you to fulfill your purpose. Life can be tough. Decisions can be hard. The Holy Spirit will guide you in your decisions, comfort you in life situations, protect you and so much more IF you let Him. The Holy Spirit is a gentleman. He will never violate your will. He is also sensitive and will not come where He is not invited or welcome.

There are many manifestations of the Holy Spirit in the Word of God. Manifestation means appearances. The first time He appears is in Genesis 1:2 in the very beginning. The Spirit of God is hovering over the waters. After that, the Holy Spirit is frequently mentioned throughout the Bible. Job talks about the Spirit giving understanding. *"But there is a spirit in man: and the inspiration of the Almighty giveth them understanding,"* Job 32:8 KJV. Judges recounts when the Spirit aided Gideon. *"But the Spirit of the Lord came upon Gideon, and he blew a trumpet; and Abi–ezer was gathered after him,"* Judges 6:34 KJV. The Spirit filled David when Samuel anointed him. *"Then Samuel took the horn of oil, and anointed him in the midst of his brethren: and the Spirit of the Lord came upon David from that day forward,"* 1 Samuel 16:13 KJV. There are many more times the Spirit showed up in the Old Testament. See the scripture examples for more occasions the Holy Spirit graced humankind with His presence.

It's different today because of the cross of Jesus. Prior to the cross, the Holy Spirit was not yet given to God's people the way the Spirit is a gift today. *"But this spoke he of the Spirit, which they that believe on him should receive: for the Holy Ghost was not yet given; because that Jesus was not yet glorified,"* John 7:39 AKJV. Today, Holy Spirit indwells God's people. The physical body is the temple or dwelling of the Holy Spirit. So, what does it mean that your body is the temple? Does it mean you are possessed like in the movies? No, not at all. This word temple is the same word used to describe the Holy Place and the Holy of Holies that were part of the design of the Hebrew temple. It is the part of the temple where God resides. It is the place where the Holy Lampstand which is the light of God, the Table of Shewbread which represents communion with God, the Altar of Incense which is the praise and worship of God, the Ark of the Covenant where the mercy of God resides, and The Holy Spirit live with you.

"What? know you not that your body is the temple of the Holy Ghost which is in you, which you have of God, and you are not your own?" 1 Corinthians 6:19 AKJV.

"For you are the temple of the living God. As God has said: "I will dwell in them and walk among them. I will be their God, and they shall be My people," 2 Corinthians 6:16.

It's important to know the Holy Spirit will never violate your will. He only lives in you if you ask, and it's really as simple as that. If you want the empowerment and help of the Holy Spirit, then just ask and receive. If you don't want it, then don't ask and He will not breach your choice.

Holy Spirit seals the believer as a guarantee of the security of salvation. He is the seal or promise that salvation is real and it's for you. Back when there were kingdoms with kings and queens where monarchs ruled, an imprint from the king's signet ring in hot wax sealed important documents. The seal was not to be broken. The Holy Spirit is certainly not wax, but He is the mark of God that promises His word is true. He is hope, life, and with you in every moment—Yes, every moment. He is the manifestation of God's promise that seals your salvation.

"In whom you also trusted, after that you heard the word of truth, the gospel of your salvation: in whom also after that you believed, you were sealed with that Holy Spirit of promise," Ephesians 1:13 AKJV.

Baptism in the Holy Spirit

Baptism in the Holy Spirit is the baptism described in the Bible as being **"filled with the Spirit."** Remember that you are a three-part being. You are a spirit that has a soul which lives in a body. You are spirit, soul, and body. It is the infilling of your spirit with the Spirit of God, which empowers you to fulfill everything God has called you to be and do.

What is the Baptism in the Holy Spirit and Why Do I Need It?

The baptism in the Holy Spirit or being filled with the Spirit is a gift. John the Baptist promised this gift when he prophesied the coming of the Messiah: *"I indeed baptize you with water unto repentance: but he that cometh after me is mightier than I, whose shoes I am not worthy to bear: he shall baptize you with the Holy Ghost, and with fire,"* Matthew 3:11 KJV. Jesus confirmed this promise when He promised living water—the Holy Spirit—to flow from believers. *"He that believeth on me, as the scripture hath said, out of his belly shall flow rivers of living water. (But this spake he of the Spirit, which they that believe on him should receive: for the Holy*

Ghost was not yet given; because that Jesus was not yet glorified.)" John 7:38-39 KJV. Jesus promised again before He ascended into heaven the baptism of the Holy Spirit. *"For John truly baptized with water; but ye shall be baptized with the Holy Ghost not many days hence"* Acts 1:5 KJV.

It is Jesus Christ that baptizes the believer in the Holy Spirit. This doesn't mean He immerses you in water like a baptism you might see at a church. Water baptism is important. It's an illustration and an important step in your walk with the Lord showing that you believe Jesus, His death, burial, and resurrection, but this is different. This is an immersion in the Holy Spirit. A friend of mine calls it being embalmed with the Holy Spirit. The Holy Spirit flows through you and preserves you for eternal life. The baptism of the Holy Spirit brings life to a body that is dead in sin. *"I indeed have baptized you with water: but He shall baptize you with the Holy Ghost,"* Mark 1:8 KJV. ('He' in this verse is referring to Jesus.)

The Holy Spirit baptizes the believer into the body of Christ. The body of Christ is another name or reference to the children or people of God. The Holy Spirit is what everyone in Christ has in common. I have been in places where I am simply minding my business and certainly not looking for other believers such as rest stops, grocery stores, doctor's offices, and many other perfectly normal places. I'm just doing my thing. Then I run into a perfect stranger that I feel a sudden deep connection. It seems like I have known that person all my life, but I've never met them before. If I spend a moment talking to them, it has never failed to be true that they are also in the brotherhood/sisterhood of Christ. The commonality that we share is the Holy Spirit. The Spirit within them recognizes and connects to the Spirit in me. It's encouraging and a little exciting. It's almost like being part of an undercover operation. *"For by one Spirit are we all baptized into one body, whether we be Jews or Gentiles, whether we be bond or free; and have been all made to drink into one Spirit,"* 1 Corinthians 12:13 KJV.

Baptism of the Holy Spirit is for the endowment or granting of **POWER** for service. You try to do right. You try to do good things and yet you keep falling into traps, getting caught in snares and life just isn't going right. The infilling of the Holy Spirit infuses you with a power so you can do right, you can keep out of traps, and stop getting tangled in snares. The Spirit empowers you to help others find their way to Christ, and you can even help them get filled with the Spirit, too. This empowerment is available if you choose to utilize it.

"But you will receive power when the Holy Spirit comes on you; and you will be my witnesses in Jerusalem, and in all Judea and Samaria, and to the ends of the earth," Acts 1:8 NIV.

Baptism in the Holy Spirit is a baptism with fire or contagious power. That doesn't mean fire will shoot out of your fingers like the superhero Pyro. It doesn't mean you have the power to take over the world as an evil dictator. When God spoke to the Israelites from the mountain in the wilderness, He appeared as fire. Fire brings purity. It burns out all the yucky stuff and leaves a pure product. In purity, you can function more like Jesus. That's powerful. Everything you see Jesus do in the Bible; you can do too with the power of the Holy Spirit. Philip, Peter, and John experienced this when Philip preached the gospel in Samaria (the outcasts of Israel) and the word spread to Jerusalem where Peter and John preached and prayed for the people to be filled with the Holy Spirit.

"But now the people believed Philip's message of Good News concerning the Kingdom of God and the name of Jesus Christ. As a result, many men and women were baptized. Then Simon himself believed and was baptized. He began following Philip wherever he went, and he was amazed by the signs and great miracles Philip performed. When the apostles in Jerusalem heard that the people of Samaria had accepted God's message, they sent Peter and John there. As soon as they arrived, they prayed for these new believers to invite the Holy Spirit into their lives. The Holy Spirit had not yet come upon any of them, for they had only been baptized in the name of the Lord Jesus. Then Peter and John laid their hands upon these believers, and they received the Holy Spirit," Acts 8:12-17.

This experience of being baptized by the Holy Spirit can take place before or after water baptism. It can even happen at the same time. Being filled with the Holy Spirit can happen anywhere. It can happen at church, at home, in your garden, in your bathtub, in someone else's home, at a concert, or anywhere. God isn't limited to only working inside the four church walls. When the Holy Spirit first came in the book of Acts, the people were in a room altogether, not in a church or synagogue. We don't know if they had been water baptized or not. Some of them were considering leaving the group and going back to their fishing boats, so maybe their faith was taking a hit. But something wonderful happened, and the Holy Spirit filled them up to overflowing. Jesus breathed the Holy Spirit into them just like God had breathed life into Adam in the book of Genesis.

"Again Jesus said, 'Peace be with you! As the Father has sent me, I am sending you. And with that he breathed on them and said, 'Receive the Holy Spirit'," John 20:21-22 NIV.

The Spirit filled those individuals so powerfully that thousands of people believed. Then they all went out and taught the story of Jesus, the Gospel. As a result, thousands more received the Holy Spirit. The baptism of the Holy Spirit has a way of snowballing.

Before receiving the gift of the Holy Spirit, the Disciples of Christ were performing miracles, signs, and wonders. After they received the gift of the Holy Spirit, the miracles that occurred from their ministries were amazing. Peter was so full of the Holy Spirit that as he walked down the street, people received complete healing when they would move into his shadow. That's powerful!

"And believers were increasingly added to the Lord, multitudes of both men and women, so that they brought the sick out into the streets and laid them on beds and couches, that at least the shadow of Peter passing by might fall on some of them. Also a multitude gathered from the surrounding cities to Jerusalem, bringing sick people and those who were tormented by unclean spirits, and they were all healed," Acts 5:14-16.

Getting to Know the Holy Spirit

Like the other two members of the Godhead, the Holy Spirit is an eternal being with unique personality traits and attributes. On the day of Pentecost, the Holy Spirit descended on Jesus' disciples. Along with His incredible power, He brought the amazing gift of grace. You can see His power and grace through His attributes, nature, and personality.

Attributes of the Holy Spirit

These four attributes are qualities that describe the Father, the Son, and the Holy Spirit. Each member of the Godhead portrays these elements.

- **Omnipotent.** Omnipotent means all-powerful, unlimited power, able to do anything. It refers to the all-encompassing power of God. The Holy Spirit has unlimited power.

"The angel replied, "The Holy Spirit will come upon you, and the power of the Most High will overshadow you." Luke 1:35.

"O Sovereign Lord! You made the heavens and earth by your strong hand and powerful arm. Nothing is too hard for you!" Jeremiah 32:17.

- **Omnipresent.** Omnipresence describes the unlimited nature of God or His ability to be everywhere at all times. The Holy Spirit is everywhere at all times.

"Where can I go from your Spirit? Where can I flee from your presence?" Psalm 139:7 NIV.

"His purpose was for the nations to seek after God and perhaps feel their way toward him and find him—though he is not far from any one of us. For in him we live and move and exist. As some of your own poets have said, 'We are his offspring'," Acts 17:27-28.

- **Omniscient.** Omniscience refers to God's superior knowledge and wisdom, His power to know all things. The Holy Spirit is all-knowing. He knows the past, the present, and the future. He knows everything about you, including your thoughts and intentions.

"But God has revealed them to us by his Spirit: for the Spirit searches all things, yes, the deep things of God," 1 Corinthians 2:10 AKJV.

"How great is our Lord! His power is absolute! His understanding is beyond comprehension!" Psalm 147:5.

- **Eternal.** Eternal means lasting forever, without time, unending. The Holy Spirit is eternal. He was, is and always will be.

"How much more shall the blood of Christ, who through the eternal Spirit offered himself without spot to God, purge your conscience from dead works to serve the living God?" Hebrews 9:14 KJV.

Personality of the Holy Spirit

The following character traits show He is not a random whisper, but a living, thinking entity. He has personality, meaning the Holy Spirit has distinctive characteristics.

- **Intellect.** The Holy Spirit is intelligent. He can look at things objectively and find the best possible answer. The Holy Spirit will teach you the wisdom of God and how to understand spiritual and natural things.

  "Which things also we speak, not in the words which man's wisdom teaches, but which the Holy Ghost teaches; comparing spiritual things with spiritual," 1 Corinthians 2:13 KJV.

- **Emotions.** The Holy Spirit experiences emotions, but His emotions do not control Him like you or I might experience. Scripture warns not to grieve the Holy Spirit of God. If the Holy Spirit can feel grief or sorrow, then He can feel other emotions as well.

  "And do not bring sorrow to God's Holy Spirit by the way you live. Remember, he has identified you as his own, guaranteeing that you will be saved on the day of redemption," Ephesians 4:30.

- **Will.** The Holy Spirit has a will. The will works with thought processes, intellect, and emotions to make choices and decisions. Will is the ability to decide on and initiate action. It is the power of choice and intention. The will of the Holy Spirit is always in accordance with the Father. He does the will of the Father at all times.

"And he that searches the hearts knows what is the mind of the Spirit, because he makes intercession for the saints according to the will of God," Romans 8:27 AKJV.

"You can ask for anything in my name, and I will do it, so that the Son can bring glory to the Father," John 14:13.

NATURE OF THE HOLY SPIRIT

The Holy Spirit is equal in His nature to the Father and the Son. Though the Holy Spirit may live with you on earth, He still has a presence in heaven since He is all-knowing and ever-present. He is in constant communication with the Father and Jesus the Son because He is an equal part of the Godhead with them. Jesus said:

"However, when he, the Spirit of truth, is come, he will guide you into all truth: for he shall not speak of himself; but whatever he shall hear, that shall he speak: and he will show you things to come. He shall glorify me: for he shall receive of mine, and shall show it to you," John 16:13-14 AKJV.

Natural eyes have seen the Holy Spirit as a separate person from the Father and Son. Each member of the Godhead has been seen on their own at different times. There is a passage in scripture, which shows all three, Father, Son, and Holy Spirit together at one time. Luke 3 shows Jesus as a man being baptized in the Jordan River. The Father opens a window in heaven and speaks to the people. The Holy Spirit descends on Jesus **LIKE A DOVE**. I don't know if the Holy Spirit actually looked like a dove or if that was the author's best description of what descended, but I know that He came like He has many times in Scripture both before and after this instance, with gentleness, peacefulness, and power. I'll leave the imagery to the deep theologians. We can see though that all three members of the Godhead were present at this event—God incarnate, Jesus Christ; The Voice of Confirmation, Father God; and the Holy Spirit like a dove.

"One day when the crowds were being baptized, Jesus himself was baptized. As he was praying, the heavens opened, and the Holy Spirit, in bodily form, descended on him like a dove. And a voice from heaven said, "You are my dearly loved Son, and you bring me great joy," Luke 3:21-22.

Here are some additional scriptures of different forms the Holy Spirit has appeared in the earthly realm. This is by far not all-inclusive. There are many more instances in both the Old and New Testaments of the visual presence of the Holy Spirit.

<u>Dove</u>: *"And Jesus, when he was baptized, went up straightway out of the water: and, lo, the heavens were opened unto him, and he saw the Spirit of God descending like a dove, and lighting upon him,"* Matthew 3:16 KJV.

<u>Water</u>: *"But whosoever drinketh of the water that I shall give him shall never thirst; but the water that I shall give him shall be in him a well of water springing up into everlasting life,"* John 4:14 KJV.

<u>Wind</u>: *"The wind bloweth where it listeth, and thou hearest the sound thereof, but canst not tell whence it cometh, and whither it goeth: so is every one that is born of the Spirit,"* John 3:8 KJV.

"And suddenly there came a sound from heaven as of a rushing mighty wind, and it filled all the house where they were sitting." Acts 2:2 KJV.

<u>Fire</u>: *"And there appeared unto them cloven tongues like as of fire, and it sat upon each of them,"* Acts 2:3 KJV.

<u>Oil (anointing):</u> *"How God anointed Jesus of Nazareth with the Holy Ghost and with power: who went about doing good, and healing all that were oppressed of the devil; for God was with him,"* Acts 10:38 KJV.

<u>Clothing</u>: *"And, behold, a woman, which was diseased with an issue of blood twelve years, came behind him, and touched the hem of his garment,"* Matthew 9:20 KJV.

<u>Seal</u>: *"Now he which stablisheth us with you in Christ, and hath anointed us, is God; Who hath also sealed us, and given the earnest of the Spirit in our hearts,"* 2 Corinthians 1:21-22 KJV.

<u>Guarantee</u>: *"Who is the guarantee of our inheritance until the redemption of the purchased possession, to the praise of His glory,"* Ephesians 1:14.

Works of the Holy Spirit

The Holy Spirit isn't just here with us hanging out. Holy Spirit plays a major role in the application of salvation. It is through the work of the Holy Spirit that draws you to Christ and fills you with gifts at salvation. It is through the work of the Holy Spirit that you have the power to fulfill your call in Christ and achieve your destiny. Following are some additional works the Holy Spirit provided to you through grace. Grace is the unmerited favor of God toward all men displayed in His general care and concern for humanity. You don't deserve grace, and yet God freely gives grace and favor. The Holy Spirit is the very essence of grace flowing through you so you can accomplish all the Lord has prepared for you. Grace encompasses so many aspects, we can't discuss them all, but here are a few gifts given to you through the Holy Spirit of Grace through His work. We will look more in-depth at individual spiritual gifts in the book *I Am Supernatural* in the *Walking with Jesus* series. The gifts listed here are gifts given to EVERYONE who receives the Holy Spirit into their lives *"And I will pour on the house of David and on the inhabitants of Jerusalem the Spirit of grace and supplication; they will look on Me whom they pierced,"* Zechariah 12:10.

Anointing. In the original Greek language of the Bible, the word anointing means to rub with oil. This is referring to a custom that came from a common practice of shepherds. Sheep can get parasites such as lice and other insects that burrow in their wool. If the insects get into the ears of the sheep, the infestation can cause death. Shepherds would rub or pour oil over the heads of the sheep so the wool was slick and the insects would just slide off and not be able to harm the sheep. Jesus is the Good Shepherd watching over you. The Holy Spirit is the anointing, which covers and protects you from spiritual parasites. The anointing also sanctifies or sets apart the person anointed. In the Old Testament, they anointed priests and/or kings for service as rulers over God's people. Anointing is for those set aside for service to God. The Holy Spirit is the anointing that sets you apart, empowers, and protects you for your walk with Christ.

"Now He who establishes us with you in Christ and has anointed us is God," 2 Corinthians 1:21.

Restraint. Grace provides the ability to restrain yourself and not fall into temptation. You can try to resist and sometimes you might succeed, but it will be super tough attempting this alone. The Holy Spirit empowers you to resist temptation, do the will of God, and make the devil run. There is one requisite: submission to God, which is also only possible by the Spirit of grace.

"Submit yourselves therefore to God. Resist the devil, and he will flee from you," James 4:7 KJV.

Conviction. The Holy Spirit brings conviction to your hearts that you might see your sin and receive the forgiveness of God. The Spirit wants you to trust and believe in Jesus Christ. He wants you to see the righteousness of Jesus so you can see your need for salvation. Conviction awakens you to your sin, the judgment for sin, and the hope of Christ. Just a reminder, conviction and condemnation are two different things. Condemnation comes from the devil and tears you down. It is a deception that points out the problem, how you failed, and what a mess you are. Condemnation is destructive and meant to separate you from God so you can't hear Him. You stop believing, stop hoping, stop being thankful, and so you stop doing God's works and break your relationship with God. Conviction, however, is from God. It is recognition of the sin committed and the opportunity to give it to God and ask His forgiveness. Instead of nagging about what a failure you are that condemnation brings, conviction calls out, "Come to Me, and I will forgive you." Condemnation shouts out the problem and makes you feel like a loser in the midst of it with no way out, while conviction provides an answer for sin and a way back to peace.

"And when He has come, He will convict the world of sin, and of righteousness, and of judgment," John 16:8.

Guidance. The Holy Spirit guides you into all truth to protect you from deception. When it gets right down to it, you are pretty helpless. It's hard to admit it, but lots of times **YOUR DECISIONS STINK**. You try to make the right choices. Choices and decisions seem right, but they turn out wrong. Remember, the Holy Spirit has the same attributes as the Father and one of those attributes is omniscience. He can see everything past, present, and future. No one can give you advice and guidance like the Holy Spirit. He will never lead you down the wrong path.

"I have yet many things to say to you, but you cannot bear them now. However, when he, the Spirit of truth, is come, he will guide you into all

truth: for he shall not speak of himself; but whatever he shall hear, that shall he speak: and he will show you things to come," John 16:12-13 AKJV.

Benevolence. Compassion and goodwill are works of the Holy Spirit. Sin makes humankind selfish and self-protective. When the Holy Spirit works through your life, then you will freely show compassion and goodwill toward others. The Holy Spirit empowers you to show love to those who are unlovable and to bless those whose intent is to harm you.

"You have heard that it was said, 'You shall love your neighbor and hate your enemy.' But I say to you, love your enemies, bless those who curse you, do good to those who hate you, and pray for those who spitefully use you and persecute you, that you may be sons of your Father in heaven; for He makes His sun rise on the evil and on the good, and sends rain on the just and on the unjust. For if you love those who love you, what reward have you? Do not even the tax collectors do the same? And if you greet your brethren only, what do you do more than others? Do not even the tax collectors do so? Therefore you shall be perfect, just as your Father in heaven is perfect," Matthew 5:43-48.

FYI: That word 'perfect' doesn't mean what you think it means. The Greek word 'teleios' is interpreted as 'perfect' in this passage. The definition of 'teleios' is to be complete, mature, and wanting nothing. **(G5046 - teleios - Strong's Greek Lexicon (KJV), 2020)** That's a little different from today's understanding of 'perfect' that can lead to perfectionism, which will create a whole list of problems. Perfectionism is often self-defeating which causes stress, anxiety, depression, and other mental health issues. **THE HOLY SPIRIT IS LEADING YOU TO MATURITY AND COMPLETENESS.**

Salvation. God does not sit back and wait to see who might accept the gift of Jesus Christ. He seeks the lost intending to bringing them to salvation and right standing with Him. Some people like to say they found Jesus. Yeah, nope. Jesus was never lost, so there was no need to find Him. People aren't really lost either, but they do lose their way. Jesus doesn't need to be found or to find you because He always knows where you are. The Holy Spirit seeks you out, enlightens your mind, confronts your sin, and inspires you to restore your relationship with the Father. One thing to remember is that the Holy Spirit never forces you to restore your relationship with God. He is gentle and kind. If you say no to God, He may increase His efforts to bring you to the Lord, but he will never force you.

"For thus says the Lord God: "Indeed I Myself will search for My sheep and seek them out. As a shepherd seeks out his flock on the day he is among his scattered sheep, so will I seek out My sheep and deliver them from all the places where they were scattered on a cloudy and dark day," Ezekiel 34:11-12.

"And this is the will of him who sent me, that I shall lose none of all that he has given me, but raise them up at the last day," John 6:39 NIV. (Jesus is talking in this passage—His goal is to lose no one that the Father gave to Him.)

Regeneration. When God created man in the beginning, He breathed life into him and Adam became a living being. Sin brought death, which once again made man an empty shell, with a death sentence. Then came Jesus. Jesus breathed new life into those who were dead in sin, but believe in Him. We call this the new birth, which is the divine side of a change of heart sometimes called conversion. You may have heard the term 'new convert' or 'new believer' or 'born again'. These terms are all speaking of the heart transformation that occurs when you accept Jesus as your personal Savior. The Holy Spirit regenerates your human spirit into a divine spirit forever linked to God.

"Not by works of righteousness which we have done, but according to his mercy he saved us, by the washing of regeneration, and renewing of the Holy Ghost," Titus 3:5 KJV.

"And the Word became flesh and dwelt among us, and we beheld His glory, the glory as of the only begotten of the Father, full of grace and truth," John 1:14.

Empowers. The Holy Spirit will lead you to a life of worship. In worship, the Spirit empowers you to live the life He has called you to live, be the person He created you to be, and to do the work He has called you to do. That's a tall order. Your past has tried to make you into something you are not. It pushed, shoved, enticed, cajoled, humiliated, and drove you into areas you never belonged. Sometimes that might look great on the outside or it might look horrible, but the common denominator is that inside misery reigns. That's because you are not living your true self. The Holy Spirit empowers you to be the true you and empowers you to tell others about Jesus and His work in your life as you transform into the real you.

"But you are not in the flesh, but in the Spirit, if so be that the Spirit of God dwell in you. Now if any man have not the Spirit of Christ, he is none of his," Romans 8:9 AKJV.

Comforts. Jesus told His disciples that He would not leave them alone when He ascended to heaven and that He would send the Comforter. The Holy Spirit is the Comforter. Comfort relieves the believer from distress. You and I both know that stress, distress, anxiety, suffering, sorrow, and pain are very much part of life. You don't have to deal with those issues all the days of your life because the Comforter is with you. If you need comfort and you need relief from any of these things, ask the Holy Spirit. He's right there waiting to love on you.

"I will not leave you comfortless: I will come to you," John 14:18 KJV.

Intercessory prayer. Prayer changes things. The Holy Spirit will plead before God on behalf of you and your situations. You may not even know what to pray. That's okay. The Holy Spirit knows what to pray. He will bring you and your situation before the throne of God for the fulfillment of God's will. That doesn't mean you do nothing. He brings those things to God through your prayers. Your responsibility is deciding to pray, opening your heart to the Lord. He will lead you and pray through you. When you are praying according to the will of God, the prayers will be powerful and the Spirit can keep you in God's will in your prayers.

"Likewise the Spirit also helps our infirmities: for we know not what we should pray for as we ought: but the Spirit itself makes intercession for us with groanings which cannot be uttered and he that searches the hearts knows what is the mind of the Spirit, because he makes intercession for the saints according to the will of God," Romans 8:26-27 AKJV.

Teaching. The Holy Spirit instructs and supervises the believer to build upon the Word of God. There are a lot of things God has told you. The Bible holds many of those things. As you read and study the Bible, your heart and mind store the truth of the scriptures. It's a lot of information and there will be some of it you just don't understand. However, when it is necessary for you to remember and understand what God has told you, the Holy Spirit will help you remember and enlighten your understanding so you can apply the truth to your life. Your job is to keep your ground fertile and pliable so the seed of the Word can grow when it's planted and be available when the Holy Spirit brings it back to you at the most opportune moment. Sin will dry up fertile ground and make it a barren wilderness. You keep your spiritual ground fertile through praise, worship, reading the Word, and prayer.

"But the Comforter, which is the Holy Ghost, whom the Father will send in my name, he shall teach you all things, and bring all things to your remembrance, whatever I have said to you," John 14:26 KJV.

Filled with the Holy Spirit

What Does that Look Like?

We have mentioned several times that the Holy Spirit will empower you. Before concluding, I want us to take a little closer look at what being empowered means. Empowerment means strength and authority are now yours to live a godly life. Being filled with the Holy Spirit is not a one-time event, it's a lifestyle. This powerful gift of the Holy Spirit is your life source for developing a closer relationship with God. The Spirit flows through you supernaturally to accomplish great things to bring God glory by fulfilling your purpose. He desires a willing and yielded vessel to flow through with freedom. This does not mean you are a puppet being manipulated by a puppeteer. You aren't a slave being driven by a slave-master. As mentioned before, the Holy Spirit will never go against your will. You can always say no. I hope you don't though. The empowerment of the Holy Spirit is evident in a surrendered life, a life freely given to God in honor and respect of the gift of salvation He gave to you. Empowerment comes to the willing and grateful servants of the Most High God.

Life changes or transformations represent an empowered life. To be continually filled with the Holy Spirit, you must be **BORN AGAIN**. To be born again means that you have repented of your sin and turned to Christ for salvation. To be born again means you believe Jesus is God born as a man, crucified on a cross for your sins, died and was buried, conquered death through His resurrection and He is coming back again.

"Now there was a Pharisee, a man named Nicodemus who was a member of the Jewish ruling council. He came to Jesus at night and said, "Rabbi, we know that you are a teacher who has come from God. For no one could perform the signs you are doing if God were not with him." Jesus replied, "very truly I tell you no one can see the kingdom of God unless they are born again." "How can someone be born when they are old?" Nicodemus asked. "Surely they cannot enter a second time into their mother's womb to be born!" Jesus answered, "Very truly I tell you, no one can enter the kingdom of God unless they are born of water and the Spirit," John 3:1-5 NIV.

Because of regeneration, given a second chance, or been born again, your life will change. The things that used to be normal for you in a state of sin won't fit anymore. You have a **NEW NORMAL**. Therefore, the believer must not continue to practice sin. That life is destroyed and a new life has begun. You have transformed into a new creation. The Holy Spirit will guide you into living a life that reflects your renewed spirit.

"But when the kindness and the love of God our Savior toward man appeared, not by works of righteousness which we have done, but according to His mercy He saved us, through the washing of regeneration and renewing of the Holy Spirit," Titus 3:4-5.

"No one born (begotten) of God [deliberately, knowingly, and habitually] practices sin, for God's nature abides in him [His principle of life, the divine sperm, remains permanently within him]; and he cannot practice sinning because he is born (begotten) of God," 1 John 3:9 AMP.

Now that the Holy Spirit has regenerated you, you can live a life that reflects Jesus. Well, you don't exactly reflect Him because you aren't a mirror. The Holy Spirit lives in you. God breathed the Holy Spirit into your life. So you aren't reflecting Jesus. You carry Jesus with you wherever you go. You are the carriers of His Light. Judges 7 tells the story of Gideon and his army who defeated the Midianite army that far outnumbered them, carrying empty clay pitchers with torches or candles in them. This is a perfect picture of you and the Holy Spirit. You are the empty clay pot. Clay because God made man from the dust of the earth. Empty when you submit your life to Christ. Empty of worry, selfishness, fear, and all things that push God out. You are clean and prepared for the Spirit of God to fill you. The Holy Spirit is the fire within you, providing light to the world. So, you aren't really a reflection of Christ. You are a carrier of the Spirit of God. You are the hands that help. You are the source of compassion. You are the one who brings the Gospel to the lost. The character of Jesus flows through you, enabling you to give up selfishness and live a life of sacrifice for others. There is an old song we used to sing in Sunday School when I was a child: ♪ "SINCE I CAME TO JESUS, ♪ FOR HEAVEN MADE A START, MY CUP IS RUNNING OVER, ♪ THERE'S MUSIC IN MY HEART, ♪ THERE'S BUBBLING, BUBBLING, BUBBLING, BUBBLING, BUBBLING IN MY SOUL. ♪" That's what it's like when you allow the Holy Spirit to flow through you. He bubbles up in your soul and spills out on everyone and everything. You are empowered to live a life surrendered to the will of God. The Holy Spirit empowers you to live a life that brings

Jesus to others in all His glory. God created you in His image. This is your opportunity to look like it.

"But whoever drinks the water that I give him will never be thirsty again. But the water that I give him will become in him a spring of water [satisfying his thirst for God] welling up [continually flowing, bubbling within him] to eternal life" John 4:14 AMP.

"But we all, with unveiled face, beholding as in a mirror the glory of the Lord, are being transformed into the same image from glory to glory, just as by the Spirit of the Lord," 2 Corinthians 3:18.

Being empowered is easy. If you want to live a life filled with the Holy Spirit, all you have to do is ask to receive him. Then just let it happen.

"If you then, though you are evil, know how to give good gifts to your children, how much more will your Father in heaven give the Holy Spirit to those who **ASK HIM***!"* Luke 11:13 NIV.

Empowerment of the Holy Spirit is not just a singular experience. It is a lifestyle choice. There is tangible evidence of the presence of the Holy Spirit. Check yourself for these signs in your life.

- The Bible describes a sign of the baptism or infilling of the Holy Spirit as the speaking of unknown tongues. This is not just random jibber-jabber, but communication and prayers coordinated by the Holy Spirit. It may sound silly and initially can feel embarrassing to your unchanged soul. The enemy will tell you it isn't the Holy Spirit, but that you have lost your mind, are being foolish, or even tricked, and that everyone is looking at you. Liturgical religion will tell you this supernatural prayer language was only for

New Testament believers. The idea that a prayer language is not for today is logic and reasoning attempting to rob you of intimate communication with the Lord. This special prayer language is a direct line of communication to the throne and carries a lot of power, so of course, the enemy wants to stop you from utilizing it. Again, the Holy Spirit will never force you. It's your choice. This is not the gift of speaking in tongues. What this is referring to is a special prayer language just between you and the Lord. That's why it's so powerful. It's prayer that the enemy can't understand. That's why the enemy hates it. He can't interpret it so doesn't know how to interfere with the request or the answer. It is Spirit-driven, Spirit-inspired, and Spirit-uttered.

"And they were all filled with the Holy Ghost, and began to speak with other tongues, as the Spirit gave them utterance," Acts 2:4 KJV.

- With the filling of the Holy Spirit, you may experience supernatural boldness and power. When the Holy Spirit filled Peter, he went right out and preached to thousands with boldness, knowing the Romans could arrest and kill him. Thousands came to Christ that day. Paul also preached to thousands while Roman guards surrounded him and thousands believed. During his incarceration for preaching the Gospel, Paul continued preaching and teaching from his prison cell. Steven gave glory to God while he was being stoned by unbelievers. You will be bold with power and confidence that defies the normal.

"But **YOU SHALL RECEIVE POWER** *when the Holy Spirit has come upon you; and you shall be witnesses to Me in Jerusalem, and in all Judea and Samaria, and to the end of the earth,"* Acts 1:8.

- Being Spirit-filled allows you to develop a deeper understanding of the Word of God. Sometimes the scriptures can be difficult to understand and even more difficult to see how stories so old can apply to your life today. The Holy Spirit opens the eyes of your understanding so you have understanding and insight of the deep lessons of God, and better know how to make decisions in your own life.

"But there is a spirit in man, and the breath of the Almighty gives him understanding," Job 32:8.

- There is the witness of Christ in you, the hope of glory. Have you ever had a moment when you just knew? **You knew** Jesus was Lord and that things would be all right, even when it didn't look like it. You knew the Father loved you. You knew a scripture was true and just for you. You just knew. Maybe you cried and dropped to your knees in humbleness. Perhaps you felt an overwhelming comfort or hope and your heart leaped with joy. Maybe mercy fell on you like a blanket making confidence welled up inside of you. That moment was a witness of Christ in you. It's mysterious and wonderful all at the same time. That moment increases your hope and is worth more than all the riches in the world.

"To whom God would make known what is the riches of the glory of this mystery among the Gentiles; which is Christ in you, the hope of glory," Colossians 1:27 KJV.

- The life you live radiates holiness and grace. Remember, holiness is pure, clean, consecrated, separated, and sacred. As a child of God, you are called to a life of holiness. As you put aside sin and selfishness and allow the Holy Spirit to fill you with grace, then you will wear holiness and righteousness like a king's robe.

"In the same way, count yourselves dead to sin but alive to God in Christ Jesus. Therefore do not let sin reign in your mortal body so that you obey its evil desires. Do not offer the parts of your body to sin, as instruments of wickedness, but rather offer yourselves to God, as those who have been brought from death to life; and offer the parts of your body to him as instruments of righteousness. For sin shall not be your master, because you are not under law, but under grace," Romans 6:11-14 NIV.

- Your actions display the Fruit of the Spirit. The Fruit of the Spirit is the Holy Spirit exhibiting the changes in you. When the Holy Spirit enters your life, your transformation begins. You go from fear to faith, anxiety to peace, anger to kindness, depression to joy, selfishness to generosity and so much more. Your life looks different and your change is out there for everyone to see.

"But the fruit of the Spirit is love, joy, peace, longsuffering, gentleness, goodness, faith, meekness, temperance: against such there is no law," Galatians 5:22-23 KJV.

- Being filled with the Holy Spirit fills your heart with thanksgiving, singing, and joy. Life has a lot of mess and can get ugly. All that mess tries to pull you into depression, ungratefulness, despair, hopelessness, and all the darkness it can muster. The Holy Spirit in you empowers you to **MAKE IT THROUGH THE DARKEST OF TIMES** and still be thankful. It can feel like all around you the world is falling apart and you still find joy. That is a power worth having

"Let the word of Christ dwell in you richly in all wisdom; teaching and admonishing one another in psalms and hymns and spiritual songs, singing with grace in your hearts to the Lord," Colossians 3:16 KJV.

- You have the opportunity for the Spirit of God to lead you. Every day you have multiple decisions to make. Some are simple and some are complicated. With the Holy Spirit, you can make your decisions with wisdom. The life choices you make in the Holy Spirit show others that you follow the Lord and belong to Him.

"Only let your conversation be as it becomes the gospel of Christ: that whether I come and see you, or else be absent, I may hear of your affairs, that you stand fast in one spirit, with one mind striving together for the faith of the gospel," Philippians 1:27 AKJV.

"For as many as are led by the Spirit of God, they are the sons of God," Romans 8:14 KJV.

- The Holy Spirit restores a right relationship with God. The Spirit working in your life is evidence that there is restoration in your relationship with God. You no longer practice sin but walk in righteousness. Circumstances no longer move you but can stand strong with the Holy Spirit giving you strength and guidance. You walk in faith instead of unbelief.

"If we confess our sins, he is faithful and just to forgive us our sins, and to cleanse us from all unrighteousness," 1 John 1:9 KJV.

Tools to Live Holy Through the Holy Spirit

To live holy, righteous, sanctified, and blessed you must develop a relationship with the Holy Spirit and allow the Holy Spirit to work through you, empowering and enabling you to fulfill the destiny and purpose of God in your life. Your relationship with the Holy Spirit is something that grows and develops each day when you implement the following in your life:

- Read and meditate on the Bible daily. (See Love Letters)

  "This Book of the Law shall not depart from your mouth, but you shall read [and meditate on] it day and night, so that you may be careful to do [everything] in accordance with all that is written in it; for then you will make your way prosperous, and then you will be successful," Joshua 1:8 AMP.

- Pray daily. (See No Secrets)

  "Pray without ceasing," 1 Thessalonians 5:17 KJV.

- Fast. {note Scripture Topic below}

"Then the disciples of John came to Him, saying, "Why do we and the Pharisees fast often, but Your disciples do not fast?" And Jesus said to them, "Can the friends of the bridegroom mourn as long as the bridegroom is with them? But the days will come when the bridegroom will be taken away from them, and then they will fast," Matthew 9:14-15.

- Fellowship with believers. You gain and give strength and insight when spending time with brothers and sisters in Christ.

    "Not forsaking the assembling of ourselves together, as the manner of some is; but exhorting one another: and so much the more, as ye see the day approaching," Hebrews 10:25 KJV.

- Maintain good works. Good works won't get you into heaven. Only belief in Christ will take you through that gate. Good works will get someone else into heaven. Your good works draw others toward Christ, opening up an opportunity for them to serve Him too.

    "And let our people also learn to maintain good works, to meet urgent needs, that they may not be unfruitful," Titus 3:14.

References

G5046 - teleios - Strong's Greek Lexicon (KJV). (2020, April 20). Retrieved from Blue Letter Bible: https://www.blueletterbible.org/lang/Lexicon/Lexicon.cfm?strongs=G5046&t=KJV

H6944 - qodesh - Strong's Hebrew Lexicon (KJV). (2020, April 8). Retrieved from Blue Letter Bible: https://www.blueletterbible.org/lang/Lexicon/Lexicon.cfm?strongs=H6944&t=KJV

H7307 - ruwach - Strong's Hebrew Lexicon (KJV). (2020, April 8). Retrieved from Blue Letter Bible: https://www.blueletterbible.org/lang/Lexicon/Lexicon.cfm?strongs=H7307&t=KJV

Stepping Stones

1. The Holy Spirit gives life as the Breath of God.

2. Father, Son, and Holy Spirit are the trinity or Godhead.

3. The Holy Spirit is the manifest presence and power of God.

4. The Holy Spirit empowers you to live the life God created you to live when you are filled with or baptized in the Spirit.

5. The Holy Spirit is omnipotent, omnipresent, omniscient, and eternal.

6. The Holy Spirit has intellect, emotions, and will.

7. The Holy Spirit is grace on earth. The power of the Holy Spirit anoints, convicts, restrains, guides, gives, regenerates, empowers, comforts, teaches, intercedes, and saves.

8. The Holy Spirit transforms your life, filling you with boldness and power.

9. Visible results of the empowerment of the Holy Spirit include the Fruit of the Spirit.

10. Tools to walking with the Holy Spirit are reading the Word, praying, fasting, spending time with other believers, and maintaining good works.

Lord, I Need Help!

WALKING WITH THE HOLY SPIRIT

1. Who are the three persons of the Trinity?

2. What does "holy" mean?

3. Describe three attributes of the Holy Spirit.

4. Name two of the works of the Spirit.

5. The Holy Spirit empowers me to...

6. How have I experienced the work of the Holy Spirit?

Glossary

SIMPLE GLOSSARY OF A FEW WORDS FROM THE CHRISTIAN FAITH

Adultery - The act of being sexually unfaithful to one's spouse

Agape - Affection, goodwill, love, brotherly love, a love feast

Angel - Messenger of God

Apostasy - Turning away from the religion, faith, or principles that one used to believe

Apostle - One sent forth, one chosen and sent with a special commission as a fully authorized representative of the sender.

Atonement - To cover, blot out, forgive; restore harmony between two individuals.

Attribute – An inherent characteristic

Backslide - To go back to ungodly ways of believing or acting.

Blasphemy - Words or actions showing a lack of respect for God or anything sacred.

Bless - To make or call holy, to ask God's favor, to praise; to make happy.

Blessing - A prayer asking God's favor for something, something that brings joy or comfort.

Born-again – To be begotten or birthed from God, the beginning, to start anew

Carnal - Of the flesh or body, not of the spirit, worldly; seat of one's desires opposed to the spirit of Christ

Cherubim - Guardian angels, angels that guard or protect places

Commitment - A promise, a pledge

Conditional - Placing restrictions, conditions, or provisions to receive

Conversion - Turn, return, turn back; change

Convert - To change from one form or use to another, to change from one belief or religion to another.

Courtship - The act or process of seeking the affection of one with the intent of seeking to win a pledge of marriage

Covenant - A pledge, alliance, agreement

Cult - A body of believers whose doctrine denies the deity of Christ.

Deliverance - A freeing or being freed, rescue; the act of change or transformation.

Demon - Evil spirit

Devil - Principal title for satan, the archenemy of God and man

Dispensation - A period of time, sometimes called ages

Dominion - To rule over, have power over, overcome, exercise lordship over

Eros - Erotic, physical love

Eternal - Existing always, forever, without time

Evangelist - Proclaims the gospel of Jesus Christ

Faith - Believing, trusting, depending, and relying on God

Fellowship - Sharing, communion, partnership, intimacy

Forgiveness - To pardon, release from bondage

Fornication - To act like a harlot, to be unfaithful to God, illicit sexual intercourse

Glorification - Salvation of the body, transforming mortal bodies to eternal bodies

Grace - Unmerited favor of God, help given in the time of need from a loving God

Holy - Set apart, sacred

Intercession - To meet or encounter, to strike upon, to pray for another

Justification - Salvation of the spirit, just as if I never sinned

Marriage - A divine institution designed by God as an intimate union, which is physical, emotional, intellectual, social, and most importantly, spiritual

New Testament - Text of the new covenant

Offering - Everything you give beyond your tithe

Old Testament - Text of the old covenant

Omnipotent - All-encompassing power of God

Omnipresent - Unlimited nature of God, ability to be everywhere at all times

Omniscient - God's power to know all things

Pastor - Shepherds of the body of believers

Philia - Conditional love, based on feelings, friendships

Praise - Thanksgiving, to say good things about, words that show approval.

Prayer - Communication with God

Prophet - One who is a spokesperson for God, one who has seen the message of God and declares that message

Propitiation - To satisfy the anger of God, to gain favor; appease

Rapture - To be carried away, or the catching away of

Reconciliation - Restore harmony or fellowship between individuals, to make friendly again

Redemption - To buy back, to purchase, recover, to Rescue from sin

Regeneration - To give new life or force to, renew, to be restored, to make better, improve or reform, to grow back anew

Repent - To give new life or force, to renew, to be restored, to make better, improve or reform, to grow back a new.

Resurrection - A return to life subsequent to death

Revelation - The act of revealing or making known

Righteousness - Right standing with God, integrity, virtue, purity of life, correctness of thinking

Sacrifice - The act of offering something, giving one thing for the sake of another; a loss of profit

Salvation - Deliverance from any kind of evil whether material or spiritual, being saved from danger or evil; to rescue.

Sanctification - Salvation of the soul. Separation from the seduction of sin

Satan - The chief of fallen spirits, opponent; adversary

Sealing - Something that guarantees, a sign or token, to make with a seal to make it official or genuine

Sin - All unrighteousness, missing the mark, wrong or fault; violation of the law

Spirit - A being that is not of this world, has no flesh or bones

Steward - A guardian or overseer of someone else's property, manager

Supernatural - Departing from what is usual, normal, or natural to give the appearance of transcending the laws of nature

Talent - A natural skill that is unusual.

Tithe - Ten percent of all your increase

Tribulation - Distress, trouble, a pressing together, pressure, affliction

Trinity - Three in one: Father, Son, Holy Spirit

Unconditional - No restrictions, conditions, boundaries, demands, or specific provisions

Will – Choice, inclination, desire, pleasure, command, what one wishes or determines shall be done

About the Author

Pamela is a teacher, mentor, and author of the inspirational book *Destiny Arise* and children's books including *Time in a Tuna*. Pam earned her bachelor's degree at the University of Illinois Springfield, her master's degree in Organizational Leadership at Lincoln Christian University, and her doctorate in Leadership at Christian Leadership University. She serves as a mentor for the Spirit Life Circles sponsored by CLU.

She works from her home in the prairie land of central Illinois. Pam and her bodybuilding husband own a gym/fitness center that promotes living a balanced life. She taught sixth grade for almost twenty years. Pam also taught preschool through adult-age students in various venues. She served as director of Super Church, the children's ministry in the United Methodist Church in her hometown. Pam also served in the church nursery, as director of New Life Ministries Discipleship Program, Vacation Bible School Director, Kingdom Kids Children's Ministry Director, and Sunday School teacher. She has also been on missionary trips. Her favorite trip, so far, was the time she spent in Belize.

Pam enjoys kayaking, bicycling, and riding her motor scooter. When she isn't writing, she enjoys spending time with her four children and their families which includes five grandchildren who are the inspiration of her children's books.

Walking with Jesus Series

BECOMING THE BEST ME I CAN BE

Book 1 - There Must Be a Better Way
Walking in Salvation

Book 2 - Lord, I Need Help!
Walking with the Holy Spirit

Book 3 - I Thought I Was Changed
Walking in Transformation

Book 4 - I Am Supernatural
Walking in Spiritual Gifts

Book 5 - I Am Strong
Walking as a Warrior

Book 6 - I Am Fruitful
Walking in the Fruit of the Spirit

Book 7 - Love Letters from God
Walking in the Word

Book 8 - Time in the Garden
Walking in the Power of Prayer

Book 9 - I'm in Charge of What?
Walking in Stewardship

Book 10 - The End of – Well, Pretty Much Everything
Walking into Eternity

Who am I? What am I doing here? Where am I going? Everyone at some point in life asks these questions. You were wired to ask and engineered to pursue the answers. The road to discovering destiny is besieged by fiascoes, failures, and the agony of defeat. If your strength has been depleted and has caused you to give up, sit down, push pause, and snooze until another day, then this book is just for you! Amazing experiences are waiting for you. Get ready to be awakened from the posture of defeat, depression, and despair.

Destiny Arise is an easy-to-read book, providing tools to aid in living an amazing life. This book is designed as a trip adviser for your expedition. It will teach you how to evict the spirit of mediocrity and use your past to propel you into your future. You will learn how to shake off the common, arising to be an uncommon force taking your rightful place in the earth. You can change the world. I pray this book will ignite a passionate fire to pursue your destiny unapologetically. Destiny, awake from your slumber and arise.

www.ingramcontent.com/pod-product-compliance
Lightning Source LLC
Chambersburg PA
CBHW062157100526
44589CB00014B/1858